Buddhism:

The Complete Guide of Buddhism

EVERYTHING YOU NEED TO KNOW TO PRACTICE
BUDDHIST TEACHINGS IN YOUR EVERYDAY LIFE

Djamel Boucly

Table of Contents

What Do We Mean When We Say Buddhism?

You may have heard that Buddhism is "one of the world's great religions"; this is a common definition of Buddhism, especially in the West, where it is likened to Christianity, Islam, Hinduism and Judaism; however, there is a major flaw in this definition: Buddhism is not a religion. Unlike religions, in fact, Buddhism does not have a dogma; Buddhism is not a belief set in stone; no Buddhist will ever tell you what you should believe in and what you shouldn't. In fact, Buddhism does not even have a god or deity of any sort. So, what is Buddhism?

Some people like to describe Buddhism as a philosophy, this is certainly closer to the truth than calling it a religion. But there is more to Buddhism than this... Buddhism is, in fact, a path to spiritual enlightenment. This path does not involve worshipping a deity, nor does it simply involve studying the truth trough philosophical spectacles (though it does do that); Buddhism is both a philosophical approach to life, reality and the universe and a set of practices that we can (but never have to) carry out in our daily lives.

In order to understand Buddhism from a western perspective, we need to realize that the mindset of the western world is divided between two main, substantially different ideologies, on the one hand, we have materialism, the belief that all that exists is matter, that there is nothing beyond what we can perceive with our senses (touch, see, smell, taste and hear), on the other hand, we have spiritualism, the belief that our physical reality is only part of what exists, and that there is much more to be discovered than what our physical senses allow. Buddhism, of course, believes that there is a spiritual reality, and gives us a path, teachings, practices to be-come fully aware of our (and of everybody's and everything's) spiritual nature.

Religions too believe that there is a spiritual realm, of course, but they also dictate what is in this spiritual realm, they state that there is a god (or more than one) who has given us a physical life and who is in charge of all reality. They are focused on worship-ping this god or gods as if he, she or they were external agents in our lives. Buddhism does not do this. So, Buddhism has been grouped together with religions simply because it is not materialist, but if you think about it carefully, you do not necessarily need to have a god to have a spirit. Ask yourself this question: can spirit exist without an overarching, all knowing and all powerful spirit? The answer is simply yes, according to Buddhism.

Does this mean that Buddhism is an atheist spiritual belief? Maybe, if you wish to describe it as such, there should not be any problem. Yet, if you come from a theist perspective, you may want to know the reasons why Buddhism does not believe in a deity. So, here they are:

• Looking at our history and development, deities seem to have been introduced into our culture to explain things that we could not explain in the past, therefore, we have Zeus, a god capable of controlling fate (or destiny) and of using thunderbolts, similarly, we have many other deities for different phenomena that now we can explain scientifically. These are normally called "gods of the gaps" because they fill in gaps in our knowledge. Buddhism does not agree with this approach, if we do not know something now, or we do not understand it, it does not mean that we will never do, in fact, our history seems to state otherwise.

• Many people turn to a deity when they face personal challenges and difficulties, how many people have turned to a god or a religious belief on their death bed, or when their lives seemed to be falling apart? According to Buddhism, this is the wrong approach: we should not look for the solution to our problems in an external agent, but within ourselves. Only by facing our own fears can we overcome them, passing the ball on to some external entity does nothing apart from removing the problem from sight and hoping that someone else will deal with it.

• The Buddha did not believe in a god or deity, this is be-cause he found no evidence of a divine power, more than two thousand years on, we still have not found irrefutable evidence of a deity.

• Some religions believe that a god is necessary to explain the creation of the universe, however, we would not need a creator if the universe had no beginning and no end. The cosmology of Buddhism, in fact, believes that while worlds (meaning temporary states of existence) have a beginning and an end (mostly described as having four phases: a creation, a duration, a dissolution and a state when they are dissolved) the universe itself, meaning all that exists, is made up of infinite sheets of these worlds, in different states of creation, therefore, while time and space are limited with-in one world, they are not in the whole of the universe. The time periods within which each world exists is called, in Buddhist philosophy, a kalpa, which is Sanskrit for "aeon" and it is believed to be a period of 4,320 million years. Worlds last for a kalpa, but as the universe itself is made up of infinite worlds, the universe is be-yond time. Modern science can only explore one world, therefore, it assumes the beginning (and end) of time and space.

Buddhism has some key teachings, which are necessary to reach spiritual enlightenment.

Karma

Karma is a very popular word, but it is sometimes misunderstood, you may have seen videos or read posts that tell you "how to use Karma to become rich" for example, the reality is not that simple. Karma is Sanskrit for "action", it means that for every choice we make there is a consequence, by controlling the choices we make in our lives, we can also direct the consequences, not just to ourselves, but to other people and the whole of the universe. However, if you think you can "use Karma" for your own inter-ests, you are mistaken, there is no way of predicting what the con-sequences of our actions will be, we cannot decide that by doing something we will get a specific reward or "punishment". Moreover, Karma depends very much on our intentions, therefore, if you do good only to get something back from it, your intention will be selfish, and it simply will not work as you would have liked.

Samsara

Samsara comes from Sanskrit too, and it can be roughly translated as either "world" or "walking", or both. The Buddhist concept of Samsara is that we are in this physical world like pilgrims on a long walk, our aim is to get to the end of this walk, but we do not know where this walk will lead us to.

Nirvana

Nirvana is yet another Sanskrit term, and a famous one all around the world, it literally means "blowing out", but it also includes the concepts of "letting go", "freedom" and in Buddhist teachings it also has a meaning of "transcendence". To transcend means to leave a state behind and move into a higher state, in spirituality, it means leaving the physical state of existence to move into the spiritual one. Thus, Nirvana is the aim of the spirit, which has been sent into the Samsara to learn, to make progress and finally find bliss and enlightenment by transcending into Nirvana. Although Nirvana has often been compared to Heaven, it is not necessarily the same, although this depends very much on how you define the word "Heaven".

The Endless Cycle of Cause and Effect

This is an important concept in Buddhism, every time we cause something, for every (even minute) action of our life, there will be an effect, yet, this effect will then be a cause in itself. This is why only by "letting go" we can achieve full bliss and transcendence.

If we do not succeed in letting go during a Samsara, we will re-incarnate, and this process will go on and on until we reach Nirvana.

The Five Delusions (also known as The Five Aggregates)

Buddhism believes that our senses are like a veil which in part reveals reality, and in part masks it as well, think about your senses as a partly see-through veil in front of you, you can only see what is behind in part, and through a filter, our senses are this very filter, they allow us to understand that there is something we can perceive, but they do not allow us to perceive it fully. Note how the word "perceive" is very close in meaning to the words "receive" and "conceive", we partly "receive" what we experience, but we cannot fully receive it, we cannot become one with it by using the senses.

According to Buddhism, there are five main deceptions:

1. Form: we can only perceive things in opposition with our senses, yellow is not red, cold is opposed to warm, the self is the opposite of what is outside oneself etc. This is an illusion given by our limited senses.

2. Feeling: this is our response to sensory perception, it is what happens inside us when we receive a stimulus from "out-side", by being reactions, feelings too are deceptions and divisive.

3. Perception: perception itself is a deception, in order to perceive something, we need to distinguish it from ourselves and from the oneness of the universe, think about how we do it in everyday life: when we say, for example, "my foot" we immediately distinguish our very foot from the rest of our body...

4. Mental Formations: our thoughts, our ideas, the concepts we use in everyday life are, our intentions create division by their own existence. When you think, for example, "I will eat that apple," you already start divining "I" from the universe, as well as from the apple itself, and the apple from the rest of the universe.

5.   Consciousness: consciousness is the ability to feel that we exist, it is the root of all our thoughts, feelings and ideas.

Mindfulness

Mindfulness is a key concept of Buddhism, mindfulness is the ability to become aware of everything, we often do things without mindfulness, we eat without being aware that we are doing it, or even being aware of the very food we eat, we drive without being aware that we are driving, we speak without being aware of who we are talking to, the list goes on and surely you can come up with many examples of yours. There are, according to Buddhism, four foundations of mindfulness:

1.   Awareness of the Body: this does not just mean your own body, but physical experience and existence as a whole.

2.   Awareness of Feelings: yet again, this does not mean your own feelings, but the feelings of every living being and of the universe itself.

3.   Awareness of Mind: not just your own mind, but the mind of others (human and not human) and of the universe.

4.   Awareness of the Objects of the Mind: the objects of the mind can be described as what our mind focuses on, these may be things or beings, but also thoughts, feelings and ideas, being aware of where our mind is focused is essential to mindfulness.

Awakening

Buddhism believes that we are asleep when we are born; you can read this metaphorically if you want. We are asleep because we are not able to connect with the universe as a whole, to experience it fully, this is due to the fact that we react (through our senses and our actions) to everything we perceive, therefore we feel our perception of the experience, not the experience itself. It is a subtle but important difference, this is the very function and meaning of Samsara, we need to awaken to the true reality beyond the veil of perception. There are 7 stages to awakening:

1.   Mindfulness.

2.   Inquiry (which means that we start investigating every-thing, and giving every experience our full attention).

3.   Infinite energy (energy is only limited within the Samsara, but we can start receiving, or sharing energy with the infinite).

4.   Joy (this is not the same as "being happy", but closer to the meaning of "bliss" which involves freedom from the material world).

5.   Tranquility (our live in the Samsara is a continuous reaction, therefore motion; tranquility can only be achieved when we do not react any more).

6.   Stillness (when tranquility becomes our very state, not just a moment in our lives).

7.   Equanimity (which means "same soul", this is when we become one with the universe, reconnecting with our transcendental nature).

Buddha

Some people may think that Buddha is the name of a person from the past, this is incorrect, Buddha means "enlightened" and "awakened". Everybody can be a buddha. We usually use the article "the" when referring to The Buddha, meaning the person or soul) born as Siddhartha who reached enlightenment and awakening, whose teachings Buddhism follows.

CHAPTER 1

Beginnings: The Buddha

It is important to know the key points in the life of the Buddha, not because we are supposed to worship him – not at all in fact – or because he is regarded as a deity by Buddhists, because his life is an example of how people can reach enlightenment and awakening, and because it is on his teachings that the whole of Buddhism is founded. Your own personal path to enlightenment may be different from that of the Buddha's, indeed, no two paths are the same, however, by knowing the steps that brought the Buddha to enlightenment, you will be able to recognize your own.

The Buddha was born Siddhartha Guatama (this was his name) into the family known as Lumbini, a royal family in Nepal. At the time, the whole Indian subcontinent was divided into many kingdoms and when his mother, the Queen, became pregnant, wise men were interviewed and they predicted that the King's son would either become the ruler of the world, if he remained a prince and then became king, or an enlightened being. We are not sure about the exact date of his birth, the Theravada school of Bud-dhism places it between 624 and 623 BCE (before Christ), but modern historians tend to believe he was born between 502 and 420 BCE. But the date is not what really matters, what matters is his journey to enlightenment, not as an end, but as a mean for us to reach enlightenment too.

Buddha's mother, Queen Maya of Shakya (this is the name of Siddhartha's kingdom) gave birth to little Siddhartha while holding onto the branches of a tree that had bent for her to give birth, Sid-dhartha's delivery into this world was fast and painless, but only seven days after his birth, she died, leaving him in the care of her sister, Mahapajapati Gotami.

Having heard the prophecy of the wise men, his father, King Suddhodana, who wanted him to take over the kingdom and be-come a great ruler, brought him up within the walls of the palace, showering him with all the luxuries available and not allowing him to see the world outside the palace wall, as he feared that if little Siddhartha, affectionately called Sakyamuni, or "the sage one of the Sakyas", saw the world outside the golden gates of the palace, where people suffered, got old and died, he would not follow into his father's footsteps. In fact, the King hold anyone who was un-well, old, or was suffering in any form from his son.

At the age of 16, Siddhartha married a beautiful woman whom he loved immensely, Yasodhara, and they soon had a beautiful son, Rahula. Pichchila - Vishada

However, Siddhartha became curious about what existed out-side the palace walls, and started to ask the King if he could go outside, at first, the king resisted, but then had to give in. Even so, he made sure that when Prince Siddhartha went outside the palace wall, old, sick and suffering people would be hidden from him, and that all the streets were swept clean. But something did not go as King Suddhodana had planned, Skyamuni saw an old man, very old, and he asked his servant what was wrong with him. His servant replied that everybody becomes old. This was the first time that Siddhartha had encountered something that was not perfect, and it had a very deep effect on him. On his second trip outside the palace walls, Siddhartha saw a sick man, he asked his servant what was wrong with him and his servant replied that everybody gets sick. On his third trip outside the palace walls, Siddhartha saw the corpse of a dead man and he asked his servant about him and his servant replied that everybody dies.

This was the beginning of Siddhartha's awakening, he realized that the world is not perfect as his father would have wanted him to believe, but full of pain, suffering and that everybody's life ultimately leads to death. For a long time after that, Siddhartha be-came sad, despondent and unhappy, nothing his father told him or gave him could make him happy, because he had realized that all the material wealth in the world was only an illusion, that we are destined to suffer and die. Once Siddhartha had seen suffering, he could not hide it from his view.

Finally, after 29 years spent in extreme luxury, Siddhartha made the momentous decision to leave the palace, abandoning his wife, father and son and going put into the world to investigate the real truth that had been hidden from him. This is not to be read as an act of cruelty towards his family, in fact, Siddhartha loved them all, but it is only by letting go of one's past, by losing every-thing, that we can reach enlightenment.

Once he left the palace, he met a group of ascetics, ascetics were, and are, people who wish to reach enlightenment by depriving themselves from all worldly goods, including food and water. So, for six years, Siddhartha almost starved himself, meditating under a tree without moving and eating only a few grains of rice a day. He was very good, naturally good at meditating, and reaching great states of focus and mindfulness when doing so, and he soon gained the respect of all the other ascetics. However, one day, as he was meditating under a tree, a beautiful girl called Sujata, who was walking by, gave him a bowl of rice and milk. That was an-other momentous incident in his life, as he realized that it is not by starving oneself that one can reach enlightenment, nor by indulging, but by what he called "the middle way", that is by seeking and achieving balance of emotions, stillness and full awareness of everything that exists.

The other ascetics were not pleased, they thought he had given up, and, at first, they refused to listen to him.

However, Siddhartha had understood that he was on the right path to enlightenment and, despite the scorn of the ascetics, he kept on his journey. One night, at the age of 35 (so soon after he had left the ascetics), as he was meditating under a Bodhi tree (a type of fig tree, with the Latin name Ficus religious, common in India) he finally reached enlightenment by making three fundamental discoveries:

He became capable of seeing all his past lives, not just as a human being, but in all forms he had incarnated before.

He became capable of perceiving all the good and evil deeds that human beings performed during their lifetimes.

He reached Nirvana, by letting go of fear, doubt, hunger, thirst, anger and desire. He knew then that his cycle of reincarnations was over, and that from then on, he would be a purely spiritual being.

This is when Siddhartha was reborn as the Buddha, the awakened one, or the enlightened one.

After having reached enlightenment, the Buddha had a choice, and he pondered over it for a few days: he could both withdraw from the world, and seclude himself from the world of suffering and death he had now conquered, or he could travel and spread his teachings, known as Dharma, so that others too could reach enlightenment. Unselfishly, he chose the second option. Thus, he gathered five of the ascetics that he had spent six years with, and gave his first sermon to them, they all saw that his middle way, the way of balance, was the right way to enlightenment and they started following him and became the first Buddhist monks. They are known as the Arhants (which can be translated as "the saints").

After this, the Buddha started travelling around the north of India on foot, covering a huge area, which is said to be 250 miles wide and 150 miles long near the Rover Ganges, in the north, where there are many forests, fierce animals and it was said that many evil spirits dwelled. He chose the darkest, most dangerous and fear ridden area of India to spread his teachings and his light. He also went back to meet his family, and his wife became the first Buddhist nun. During these years, the Buddha preached to everybody who would listen to him, he never forced his words, but soon his reputation became very well known, and people gathered to hear the Dharma of the enlightened one. Tens of thousands of people joined as his disciples, and they, too started spreading the Buddha's Dharma.

When he was about 70, after 35 years of travelling and preaching, his health began to get worse, however he kept preaching till the day he died, at the then venerable age of 80, in a small town called Kusinagara, where he left his last words, "Decay is natural to all things, make sure you strive with clarity of mind for Nirvana." Then, he assumed the lion's position and passed on peacefully.

During his preaching years, the Buddha left the Vinaya, a code of practice for Buddhist monks and nuns still in use nowadays, you do not need to be a monk or a nun to be a Buddhist, this code is just for them. He, of course, also left his Dharma, his teachings. However, the Buddha never chose a successor and never wrote down his teachings. It was only 250 years after his death that Buddhist monks gathered in council collected and wrote down all his teachings in a book known as the Tripitaka. The Tripitaka also includes many commentaries and traditions, known as the Sutras (Sanskrit for "discourses").

CHAPTER 2

Different Buddhist Traditions: How We Act on Our Practice

The first thing to understand about practicing Buddhism is that, unlike many religions and spiritual practices, it does not require a mechanistic approach. Mechanistic means that some rituals are requested at given moments or in given situations, one just has to attend Mass to realize that there are set actions to be carried out at exact moments and with prescribed actions, these may go from singing specific hymns, to doing the sign of the cross at precise moments, to dipping one's fingers in the font on entering a church to genuflecting during the Eucharist. As you can see, a specific moment requires a specific ritual. This does not happen in Buddhism. In fact, Buddhism is a teaching that allows you to practice it in your own chosen way. No two people are the same, therefore, no two paths to Nirvana are the same either.

Buddhism does not prescribe, it only suggests.

People are fully free to choose which suggestions they want to follow when to do so, how frequently and in which specific way. You don't have to, for example, meditate to follow Buddhism. You don't have to chant mantras, nor visit a Buddhist temple at any given time... It is up to you to choose how you go about it.

What really matters in Buddhism is your intention, if you can-not practice on one day, maybe because you have no time (mod-ern life can be very hectic indeed!), you have no one to answer to for this. However, although we cannot say that there is a "good Buddhist" and a "bad Buddhist" because Buddhism has no dog-ma (while often people are defined as, for example, "good or bad Christians" according to how closely they follow their religion's dogma), if you want to reach enlightenment, you need to have some consistency. The fact is that if you don't reach enlightenment in this life, the only consequence is that you will reincarnate again, and this will continue until you have finished your journey. There is no damnation if you "fail", in fact, there is no failure altogether.

However, you need to understand that the key aim of Buddhism is to avoid Karmic problems (by hurting others) and aiming for Karmic benefits (by helping others). Therefore, tolerance is key to Buddhism, it does not matter if you understand others (and this does not include only human beings, as we will see), you should never hurt others.

There are, as we will see in the next chapter, different schools of Buddhism, but all will expect you to consider the Karmic con-sequences of your actions before you act, you will have to keep an eye into the future and every time you do something, ask yourself what consequences may come of it, if you are aware that your actions may hurt someone, then you should desist. If you are not aware of possible negative Karmic consequences, but later on be-come aware of them, you should be learning a lesson from it, and by doing so learn to see deeper and deeper into the future.

As we said, what matters in Buddhism is intentions.

Buddhism is a way of living, it cannot be taken as being a ritual performed on a certain day, or at given times during the day, practicing Buddhism means changing the way you co duct your-self in everyday life, always considering the effects that your actions (thoughts and feelings) have on other beings and on the universe itself. If you fail, be aware that you are only human, and you are not perfect, as you should not judge others for failing, neither will you be judged if you do. However, this should not be an excuse, you should always strive to reach enlightenment. It is the striving that matters most in Buddhism.

Naturally, there are practices in Buddhism that will help you become more attuned with the spiritual reality of the universe and will enhance your awareness and mindfulness, most people choose to carry out all of these practices, within their own abilities (re-member, there is no obligation) and some of the key ones are as follows.

Meditation

Meditation is key to all Buddhist schools, it is essential to reach mindfulness, to awaken and to become enlightened. You do not need to practice meditation for long periods of time, it all depends on how busy your life is and how many engagements you have. A meditation session, however, should last about 20 minutes mini-mum (but there is literally no limit to how long it can be, in fact, some monks can meditate for many days on end). The key to meditation is to make your mind still, this is important especially in western societies and in urban areas, where our mind is forced by the pace of life to keep moving, to keep shifting focus from one thing to another. The key to meditation is to get the ego silent, the ego speaks to us continuously, it is that voice at the back of our mind that keeps talking to us. Therefore, to practice meditation, you have to be relaxed, comfortable, in a comfortable and quiet place (though expert meditators can meditate anywhere) and start focusing in your breathing. We will look at specific meditation techniques later in this book. At this stage, though, you may want to set aside some short periods of time during the day or during the week which you can dedicate to meditation.

Prayers

Prayers are not a necessity in Buddhism, some Buddhist schools, for example Theravada, are actually skeptical of prayers, because they are particular about how Buddhism does not believe in a deity, and prayers often turn into acts of worship. Not even the Buddha should be worshipped. However, other schools of Buddhism, for example Tibetan Buddhism, value the role of prayers as a way of communicating with the universe. It is up to you to choose whether to pray or not, and maybe the next chapter will make your choice clearer, as we will be talking about the three main schools of Buddhism. Remember, however, that if you choose to pray, you do not need to stock to formulas (as happens instead in many religions), Tibetan Buddhism stresses how it is important that a prayer sends one's personal wishes to the universe, and it also stresses how the number of prayers is important.

Chanting

Chanting is very common in Buddhism, it originated in India and has become a central practice in Zen. Chanting brings peace to the spirit, and it connects you to the universe through sound. Buddhism believes that sounds are absolutely essential to connect with the spiritual reality. There are many tried and tested chants in Buddhism, which send our vibrations into the cosmos, they basically speak "the language of the universe", which is all waves of energy beyond its physical appearance. Maybe the most famous chant is the "aum" chant, which is believed to be a link to the ancestral soul of the universe. You can chant individually or collectively, it is believed that collective chants have much more power than individual ones, and this is why Buddhist monks often engage in collective chanting.

Vegetarianism

Buddhism does not impose vegetarianism, but as Buddhism believes that there is spirit in everything, and as we know that animals are sentient beings, killing them for our own interest is negative in terms of Karma. We should not hurt anything, and in order to eat meat, we certainly hurt another being. It is not easy to be-come a vegetarian in many cultures, the meat industry is very powerful and centuries of tradition are not easy to overcome. However, do not believe that you cannot live without meat, in fact, vegetarianism (and veganism in particular) is much healthier than eating meat, all studies show this. We are not, and never have been, made to be meat eaters, our canines are very small (like in most herbivores), we do not sweat from our tongue (all carnivores do), we can move our jaws sideways (only herbivores do that), our stomach has the exact length of a herbivore's, we actually cannot digest animal proteins well (they increase the acidity of our stomach and body, we simply do not have the enzymes to digest them). We as a species have lost contact with our real, herbivorous nature.

If you decide to become a vegetarian and are not one already, do it in small steps, it is easier to succeed by taking it slowly. Re-member that many vegetables have a much higher protein content than any type of meat, and these proteins are actually much healthier than meat ones. Maybe the most difficult thing in be-coming a vegetarian is the pressure of family, friends and society in general. Most people who have given up meat and fish do not miss them, however, it can be difficult to go to a dinner party and be a vegetarian, and it is sometimes very difficult to "come out" as a vegetarian to one's parents.

CHAPTER 3

Theravada, Mahayana and Vajrayana

As we have said in previous chapters, there are different schools in Buddhism; if you are new to Buddhism, you do not need to choose any of them, as you become more acquainted with this spiritual practice, you will find the school that best suits your own path. In this chapter, we will look at three very popular and important schools of Buddhism: Theravada, Mahayana and Vajrayana.

Theravada

Theravada is a very old school of Buddhism whose name comes from two Sanskrit words, thera, meaning "elders" and vada, meaning "word" and it is vaguely translated into "the word of the elder monks". This is because it follows the teachings of the Pali Canon, a collection of scriptures composed in North India in 29 BCE by the Fourth Buddhist Council, this is approximately 454 years after the death of Guatama Buddha (the "physical Buddha" or the "historical Buddha"). Theravada is strictly non-theistic, meaning that it focuses on the non-existence of a deity and it is regarded as a "conservative" or "traditional" form of Buddhism. It is very common in many countries, especially in Thailand, Sri Lanka, Laos, Cambodia, Malaysia and Nepal, as well as in other countries as a minority school of Buddhism.

There are some key principles that Theravadins (people who follow Theravada) believe in:

Arhats (a word that we can see means roughly "saint", but more correctly "worthy ones" or "perfect ones") are perfect (other schools suggest that arhats can "regress" meaning that they are between the physical life and the spiritual one, which makes them capable of still making mistakes).

Insight is sudden, unlike other schools, which believe that insight and enlightenment happen gradually, Theravada believes that they happen suddenly (a bit as it happened to the Buddha), this does not mean that one day, without having ever walked the path to enlightenment, you will reach insight, but that the change from a state of sleep to one of spiritual wakefulness will happen suddenly, when the balance between your physical nature and your spiritual one tips over.

Insight comes from vibhajjavada, vibhajjavada means "teaching and learning of analysis". Theravada believes that it is by developing your critical understanding that you will be reaching wisdom and enlightenment. Learning is therefore fundamental to Theravada.

The path to purification has seven stages:

Sila-visuddhi, or purification of your personal conduct in life.

Citta-visuddhi, or the purification of your mind and thoughts.

Ditthi-visuddhi, or purification of your perception (or view).

Kankha-vitarana-visuddhi, or reaching purification by overcoming doubt (and with it, fear).

Maggamagga-nanadassana-visuddhi, which means that purification, at this stage, comes through the knowledge and vision of what is the path and what is not the path, it is when people realize where their path is leading them and start following it.

Patipada-nanadassana-visuddhi, which means that purification comes from the knowledge and perception (or vision) of how the path unfolds in practice, in your daily life, in every action and choice that is presented to you.

Nanadassana-visuddhi, which is purification by pure knowledge and perception, this is the culmination of the path, which will result in sudden insight and Nirvana.

According to Theravada, in order to become enlightened, we need to understand the three characteristics of all sankhara (which means "conditioned phenomena"), sankhara is a very important concept in Theravada, as it is at the root of Karmic events, all Karmic events have three key characteristics which we need to understand in order to analyze them and then act upon them in order to make the right Karmic choice, this is at the very core of the teachings of Theravada, we said before that it is through learning (and wise teaching) that one can reach enlightenment according to Theravada, learning about the quality of Karmic events is therefore fundamental to our path to enlightenment. Here are the three key qualities of all Karmic events:

Anicca; this means that all Karmic events are temporary and impermanent, everything changes. In order for something to be eternal and permanent, it would need to have an eternal and permanent cause to it, instead, if we look at our lives, we can notice that everything is in continuous motion. When something happens to us ("good" or "bad", it does not matter), we know that it will not last forever, this includes when things that shake our life happen, we may assume that they will last forever, but they don't.

Dukkha, this can be translated into "suffering", suffering comes from craving. We suffer because we crave for something which we do not have. If you are craving for a different job, a partner, a better house, health or money, this is where suffering comes from. Whenever we decide that we like or dislike something, we create suffering for ourselves and for others, because we start craving.

Anatta, this is a Sanskrit word which means "not self". The idea of self is a deception, this applies to both phenomena and beings, in fact, it is impossible to define what "self" actually means...

Atta (Self)

It is important to see why Theravada does not believe that the self exists, in fact, according to Theravada, the idea of self is one of the biggest illusions, or deceptions, in our Samsara. According to Theravada, we are made up of five elements, or aggregates (khandhas in Sanskrit), these are as follows:

Rupa (our physical form)
Vedana (our sensations and feelings)
Sanna (our senses, our perception)
Sankhara (our thoughts and ideas, our mental formations)
Vinnana (our consciousness)

However, none of these can be identified as the self. Every khandha is perpetually and continually changing, our body changes all the time (just think about the billions of cells that are replaced every minute), our feelings change all the time, our ideas change all the time etc... Therefore, there is no such thing as self.

Kilesas

Kilesas are defined as "defilements", these are the very causes of the cycle of death and rebirth, they are at the root of our Karmic actions with negative consequences to ourselves and others, and they all originate from avijja (or ignorance), note that ignorance does not just mean "rational ignorance", when we hurt a being, this may come from the inability to empathize with this being, for example, which is ignorance. Ignorance is also the state we are in when we are born, we do not know our previous lives and we do not know our role in this world, therefore, our duty is to conquer this ignorance and in doing so, as we understand how Karma is working on our lives, we can make the right choices and we can then reach Nirvana. Theravada identifies five panca nirvana (five hindrances to the path to Nirvana) which slow down or stop our path towards enlightenment:

Kamachhanda, or sensory desire.
Vypada, or evil intent.

Thina-middha, or dullness, omission.

Uddhacca-kukkucca, which means continuous worry, the inability to calm our mind.

Vicikiccha, which is doubt.

In order to overcome these hindrances, we need to use meditation, which calms the mind and allows us to achieve higher and higher states of consciousness, or jhanas.

Mahayana

Mahayana is the most common form of Buddhism around the world, it is calculated that more than 50% of Buddhists follow Mahayana. It comes from the Sanskrit words maha, meaning "great" as in Mahatma (great soul), and yana, meaning "vehicle" and it is translated as "the great vehicle". Mahayana top, like Theravada seeks Bodhisattva, which means "full enlightenment", but it offers a different path to it. Mahayana is very popular in India, China, Bangladesh, Taiwan, Indonesia, Mongolia, Japan, Vietnam, Bhutan, Nepal, Korea and Malaysia. Japanese Zen, for example, can be classed as part of Mahayana. The key texts of Mahayana are the Mahayana Sutras, the Agama and commentaries known as the Mahayanasamgraha.

At the core of Mahayana there is the belief that releasing and overcoming suffering to reach Nirvana and Bodhisattva is not enough. You can see where this is coming from if you think about what may happen if you just overcome suffering, true, you will not have any negative Karmic consequences, which indirectly will influence others, as well as yourself, however, is it possible to have an actively positive effect on Karma? This is what Mahayana sets out to achieve. This can only be achieved, according to Mahayana, by reaching Trikaya, or full and omniscient Buddhahood. This can only occur when we achieve Prajna, or transcendent wisdom, the wisdom that allows us to understand the full workings of Karma, not just as they appear in our Samsara, in our existence in this world, but beyond this, into the spiritual realm. In order to do this, we will need six paramita (roughly translated as "perfections" which will allow us to achieve Bodhisattva and Bodhicitta (an enlightened mind, the key quality of a buddha).

Paramita (Perfections)

Here are the five perfections which we need to strive to achieve:

Dana-paramita, this means the perfection of giving, not giving to have something in return, but giving for giving's sake.

Sila-paramita; this means achieving perfection of conduct, behavior and self-discipline.

Ksanti-paramita; the ability to achieve forbearance, which is tolerance, restraint and patience.

Dhyana-paramita; this is perfection of meditation, therefore the ability to reach high levels of consciousness through it, a bit like the Buddha did in his lifetime.

Prajna-paramita; this is transcendent wisdom.

Upaya (the Means) and the Lotus Sutra

In order to achieve Buddhisattva, Mahayana follows the teachings of the Lotus Sutra, this follows the Eightfold Path, which will be exploring more in detail in a future chapter, each step of the path is a "mean" to enlightenment, not the end and these means are called upaya:

Right view or perception
Right resolve or intention
Right speech
Right conduct
Right livelihood
Right effort
Right mindfulness
Right concentration (samadhi in Sanskrit)

Right view and right resolve are part of wisdom, right speech, right action and right livelihood are part of moral virtue, right effort, right mindfulness and right concentration are part of meditation. Wisdom, moral virtue and meditation are known as the three divisions of the eightfold path of Mahayana.

Liberation

Liberation from Samsara may not occur within a lifetime, this goes back to the principle of Buddhism that we will be within the cycle of reincarnations until we reach Nirvana. Whether a follower reaches Nirvana during a specific lifetime depends on many factors, including how far she or he is on the path to enlightenment when she or he incarnates and, of course, this person's actions and intentions during the specific lifetime. However, even if we may not be reaching Nirvana in this Samsara, or lifetime, we can make progress in this lifetime so that at the next we will start closer to Nirvana. This is a very important concept of Mahayana. For many people, especially in the West, who have grown up believing that this is the only life we have, and this is the only chance we have to go to Heaven or Hell (this is the metamyth of the West, meaning the underlying ideology of all western cultures), this may be a difficult concept to come to terms with, as many westerners will feel that they have to "accomplish" within this specific lifetime.

Buddha-dhatu

Once a person reaches enlightenment, she or he has achieved Buddha nature (or Buddha-dhatu). Everybody can reach this state (though not all Mahayanists agree on this). Basically, the idea is that when we are born, each one of us is endowed with a bodhi, or a direct link to dhatu, also known as "the uncreated element" that is the real essence of our being. Our role in this Samsara is therefore not to find, or to produce a new nature for ourselves, but to rediscover our own dhatu through the bodhi. Once we become aware of, once we rediscover and get to know our dhatu, we can reach Nirvana. Bodhi can be roughly translated into "a state of being awake" or "awakedness", thence the term "awakening". This awakening can only occur, a cording to Mahayana, via sunyata, which means "emptiness", by which it is meant that we need to empty ourselves of all the negative behaviors, thoughts, feelings and intentions (klesas in Sanskrit) that form a veil between ourselves and our real, spiritual and enlightened nature.

Vajrayana

Although Vajrayana is sometimes regarded as part of Mahayana, some scholars regard them as separate and this is how we will be considering them in this book (though the classification is not what matters). Vajrayana is again a Sanskrit term which is not that easy to translate, it comes from vajra, which literally means "thunderbolt" and yana, which we have already seen means "vehicle", however, the two words combined mean "diamond vehicle" or "bright vehicle". It is regarded as the tantric school of Buddhism, in fact it is also called Tantrayana. Tantra is not unique to Buddhism, it is in fact, the belief that we can channel divine, universal energy into our microcosm. Tantrayama is the least popular if the main schools of Buddhism, in fact it only practiced by roughly 6% of Buddhists.

It is an extremely complex philosophy and practice so in this book we only have time to look at its basic principles.

Bodhisattva

Vajrayana too aims to give a path to Bodhisattva, but this is done through what is known as the path of the fruit, the idea is that our bodhi is inside of us, in the same way as a fruit is inside every seed of a fruiting tree. Think about it, when you plant a peach, for example, what you do is put a kernel in the ground, but doesn't that kernel already possess all the potential to become a big tree and to bear fruit? So, if when we are born we already own a bodhi, would it not be logical that our role in this Samsara is to grow like trees and allow our bodhi to express its full potential?

Samaya (Tantric Vows)

Vajrayana believes that in order to allow ourselves to express our bodhi fully and reach Buddha-dhatu, we need to uphold fourteen vows, known as tantric vows:

Never disrespect the Vajra master.
Never transgress the words of the Buddha.
Never insult your vajra brothers and sisters.
Give abandoning love to all sentient beings.
Abandon yourself to the bodichitta in intention and behavior.
Do not criticize the sutras and tantras.
Do not reveal secrets to those who are unworthy.
Do not mistreat your body.
Do not reject emptiness.
Do not keep bad company.
Do not fail to reflect on emptiness.
Do not upset those who have faith in the Dharma.
Do not fail to observe your samaya commitments.
Do not denigrate women.

As you can see, Vajrayama is a bit different form other forms of Buddhism, to start with, it is esoteric, this means that you have to be "initiated" (meaning taught) to practice it, secondly, it has strict rules that you need to observe, you cannot divert from these rules, or vows with any of the three Vajras (body, mind and spirit).

If you make a mistake, you can still reach enlightenment, but this depends on how big and radical the mistake is, this is seen, again, through a metaphor that involves trees: if a branch is damaged, it can grow back again, but if it has been completely severed off, it will not be able to grow again, moreover, even if the damage is small, if we do not look after it and repair in in due time, the damage will become unrepairable. Replace the branches with the samaya and yourself with the tree and you will see that if you commit a mistake, you will be able to make reparations only if the mistake is not drastic, and only if the branch has not be damaged beyond repair, and you act upon your mistake within reasonable time (which is believed to be three years). However, if you allow the damage to continue to any one of the branches, the whole tree will become weaker, until the roots themselves will weaken and the tree will die.

Tantra

Of course, tantra is at the very heart of Tantrayama, thus, it is important to understand what the tantric techniques of Vajrayana are.

There are four levels of tantra, in a hierarchy:

Kryayoga, this is the lowest level of tantra and it occurs through actions and rituals.

Chryayoga, this is the second level of tantra and it takes place through meditation.

Yogatantra, this is a higher level of tantra that we can practice through yoga.

Anuttarayogatantra, this is the highest form of yoga tantra.

Kryayoga, Chryayoga and Yogatantra are regarded as "outer tantras", but Anuttarayogatantra is "inner tantra", this is in itself divided into three types of tantra: Mahayoga (which is used to foster development), Anuyoga (which develops practice and perception) and Dzogchen (translated into "great perfection", which allows us to connect with the divine and universal and our true nature). As you must have noticed, yoga is very important in Tantrayana, in fact, many people practice yoga both in the East and in the West, but in order to practice yoga for Vajrayana, you really need to do it very regularly and progress from simple forms of practice to very difficult and complicated ones. This may be one of the reasons why Vajrayana is not the most widespread form of Buddhism.

While practicing yoga, followers of Vajrayana need to discover and practice the four purities:

Perceiving your body as the body of the deity, of the whole.
Perceiving your environment as the mandala (the pure land) of the deity.
Perceiving your enjoyment as the free bliss of the deity.
Performing your actions not for your own good, but only for the good of others.

As you can see, while Buddhism in general is not theistic, Vajrayana is, it does not define the deity, it doesn't tell us what the deity's name is etc, but it assumes that there is a universal deity which acts through us, and it is only by allowing this deity to take full control over us that we can reach enlightenment.

If you are new to Buddhism, you do not need to choose a school of Buddhism to start with, but hopefully, this exposition of the three main schools of Buddhism will have helped you identify the one that best suits you, they all follow the teachings of the Buddha, but their focus is different, moreover, because Buddhism, unlike religions, does not prescribe a dogma, the choice is fully yours, and you should be choosing according to where you think you are in your path to enlightenment and by selecting the school that you think will help you better in your path.

CHAPTER 4

Chinese Buddhism

In China, Buddhism is very popular, the most common school of Buddhism in China is Mahayana, and the history if Chinese Buddhism is very ancient indeed. Buddhism is believed to have reached China in the third century BCE, where the atmosphere was ripe for this spiritual practice, which mixed with the indigenous Taoism, Tao-ism derives its name from Tao, believed to be the source or eternal principle of all creation. It is to Taoism, for example, that we owe the concept of Yin and Yang, Taoism believes that we should be finding a path, a way, to live in harmony with creation. It is there-fore not difficult to see how Buddhism became popular in this country very early on. Despite original opposition from the ruling dynasty, to the point that the Qin Emperor ordered the full annihilation of Buddhism in 213 BCE. However, thanks to the Silk Road, the road that even in antiquity linked Asia to Europe through India, Buddhism returned and prospered in China. Again in 845 AD, (or CE, as it is now called), the Tang Dynasty ordered the destruction of thousands of Buddhist temples and monasteries. But Buddhism came back into China through the Chama Road, a commercial route that linked China and India, and by the now famous Ming Dynasty (1368 to 1644 CE), Buddhism had become very popular in China. It is now a major influence on all aspects of Chinese life, despite the Communist regime, which, un-like in Russia, never obliterated, but rather incorporated, indigenous spiritual practices.

It is actually through China that Buddhism eventually reached Japan (see the next chapter) where Zen Buddhism was developed, which then came back into China where it is now extremely popular as well.

Because Chinese Buddhism merges with Taoism, although its core principles are the same as those we explored in the previous chapter, it also has its own traditional ritual and practices.

Incense Burning

Incense burning is typical of Chinese Buddhism; this practice comes from the belief that burning wood creates a bridge between the physical and the spiritual realms; originally, scented woods were burnt, but this later on developed into burning sandalwood. Buddhist monks have since discovered that burning incense in-creases their concentration and mindfulness.

Chinese Festivals

Chinese Buddhism also has its own specific festivals, there are really many of them, but some are more famous and important than others, for example:

• On the eighth day of the twelfth month if the Chinese calendar, they celebrate the enlightenment of the Buddha.
• On the first day of the first month of the Chinese calendar, they celebrate the birth of the Mayatera Buddha (roughly translated as "the Buddha of the future" as they hold the eschato-logical belief that the Buddha will return).
• On the eighth day of the second month of the Chinese calendar, they celebrate the renunciation of the Sakyamuni Buddha.
• They have four different festivals for the birthday of the Bodhisattva.

Laypeople

In Chinese Buddhism, laypeople play a much bigger role than in Buddhism in other areas, for example in Tibet. This has been popular since the times of the Ming Dynasty and there are many revered laypeople in their tradition, and laypeople have been helping develop meditation, mindfulness and mantra recitation.

They also have some specific incarnations of the Buddha (the Medicine Buddha, or the Buddha seen as the enlightened being who cures from suffering, for example, which is originally from China).

Other Chinese Buddhist Beliefs and Rituals

Apart from burning incense when praying and meditating, Chinese Buddhism is also characterized by the following:

- A belief in reincarnation.
- The belief that religious ceremonies and rituals can help the souls of people (especially dead people) find peace.
- A belief in the existence of ghosts.
- A belief in the existence of Hell.
- The traditional Quingming festival, where people pay their respects to their ancestors.
- Prayers are given to a series of deities in the realm of Heaven.
- The belief that people will be drawn to each other in this life through affinity.
- A belief in retribution for the actions we perform in this life.
- Vegetarianism and the need to be compassionate towards all living souls.

As you can see, Chinese Buddhism differs quite significantly from other forms of Buddhism, as it mixes different traditions, pays a lot of attention to rituals and festivals and has a strong focus on death and the afterlife, which is absent in other forms of Buddhism.

CHAPTER 5

Japanese Buddhism

As we said in the previous Chapter, Buddhism reached Japan from China in the 6th Century CE (or AD), by 552 CE, it had reached the Land of the Rising Sun, during the Kofun period. There, it developed into many schools which have been teaching the Dharma ever since. The main schools of Buddhism in Japan are Jojitsu, Hosso, Sanron, Kegon, Risshu and Kusha-shu, and two esoteric schools, Tendai and Shingon, which are collectively known as the Nara Schools, on top of these, there are the Kamakura Schools, which include the Amida School and Zen. We cannot go into the details of each school in this book, but we can look at the general characteristics of these schools.

Nara Schools of Buddhism

These are the oldest schools of Buddhism in Japan, and they became established in the seventh and eighth centuries AD (or CE), they take their name from the city of Nara, which was then the capital of Japan. These schools were sponsored by the imperial court, and in fact this is reflected in their temples, which are very rich in paintings and statues. There are now 400 Nara temples in Japan, and the Nara schools have roughly 2.5 million followers.

The history of the Nara schools of Buddhism in Japan is closely linked to the country's history, they had a peak between the eighth and the twelfth centuries, when they achieved dominance through the support of the imperial family, but have declined since.

Nara Buddhism has had a deep impact on the arts and literature of the country, Nara temples and monasteries survive to the present day, and they show a strong influence of Chinese Buddhism.

During what is known as the Nara period, monasteries accumulated a vast amount of land and power, and it was during this period that Buddhism became the official religion of Japan. The most active promoter of Buddhism during this period was Emperor Shomu, who ruled between 729 and 749 CE (or AD), during his reign, Japan was hit by a series of disasters, including famine and drought, the Emperor saw Buddhism as a way of bringing prosperity and unity back into the country, and set out on a colossal endeavour to build temples, monasteries and pagodas, during his reign alone, more than 200 temples were built.

Nara Buddhism is not strictly atheist, in fact, following the lead of China, it incorporates deities into its spiritual practice, the Emperor commissioned innumerable statues in bronze, in clay, in wood and in lacquer to be placed in the many temples that had been built. Arguably the most famous statue from the period is the bronze Buddha at the Todai-Ji temple known as Daibutsu Buddha, this was erected to give protection and prosperity to Japan.

Ironically, while the famine and droughts ended, and Buddhism did bring unity to Japan, the huge building enterprise also depleted the imperial coffers of precious metals, and ultimately bankruptcy.

Kamakura Schools of Buddhism

Kamakura Buddhism became established in Japan in the twelfth century, mainly thanks to the charisma of its teachers, this period is known in Japanese history for the establishment of the Shogun, the Shogun, in Japan, became the effective ruler of the land, while the Emperor remained as a "divine ruler" with mainly ceremonial functions. Japan basically turned into a military dicta-torship, which lasted from 1192 to 1867 AD (or CE). It is during what is known as the Kamakura period that Japanese Buddhism took on specific characteristics which last till today, and which are also a fundamental part of Zen, these are characterized by the non-adherence to some traditional Buddhist practices known as the sila:

The sila forbade monks from engaging in sexual practices, but in Japan, during the Kamakura period, this was abandoned and monks were free to marry.

The sila prescribed vegetarianism, which was abandoned in Ja-pan, where fish and meat are still nowadays common food for monks and for laypeople alike.

The sila prohibited the consumption of alcoholic beverages to followers of Buddhism (both monks and laypeople), but this was abandoned during the Kamakura period.

The sila, especially in India, prescribed that monks could only own and wear two robes, this was abandoned by Kamakura monks, who could own as many as they wished, moreover, high ranking monks would be able to wear really elaborate and expensive robes.

For some people, Japanese Buddhism is a departure from tradition, which embraces a life of simplicity and a rejection of worldly wealth, in general, Kamakura Buddhism also broke down the distinction between layperson and monk.

Zen

Zen actually originated in China, but it became particularly popular in Japan, in fact, its name derives from the Japanese pronunciation of the Chinese word chan, which in turn comes from the Sanskrit dhyana, the word "Zen" can be roughly translated as meaning "absorption" or "deep meditation". This is why we will be talking about Zen in this chapter, and not under Chinese Buddhism, because it is the last chapter on the development of Buddhism in the East, as

Zen has traits that come from both China and Japan, and maybe it is clearer to discuss it after having learnt about Japanese Buddhism.

Zen places a lot of emphasis on meditation, it has developed many forms of meditation, including the lotus position and the half lotus position, in Zen, meditation should not be anchored, by this we mean that the mind should not be fixed on an idea or phenomenon, but it should allow itself to be guided and driven by the universe itself, the mind has to let go of its own will during Zen meditation, as its will is seen as part of the very ego that prevents enlightenment. Meditation in Zen can be very intensive, often lasting for periods of hours, and sometimes even days, it can also be done collectively.

Another important principle of Zen is koan, this is a public dis-course between a master and a follower where the follower demonstrates that she or he has understood the master's insight into the deeper truths of the universe.

Zen also has its own liturgy, which can be carried out by monks, but also by laypeople (we have seen how Japanese Buddhism has blurred the distinction between the two), in these services, carried out daily in monasteries, practitioners carry out the following:

They chant some major sutras.
They chant some minor sutras.
They give offerings to the Buddha or to Bodhisattvas.

In Japan, people have altars dedicated to family members who have dies and they give them offerings and pray for them.

The teachings of Zen are notoriously very difficult to comprehend to the western mind, this is because Zen does not believe that words are sufficient to explain the deeper truths of the universe, and their teachings are often metaphorical, a famous example is D.T. Suzuki's famous "the finger pointing at the moon remains a finger and under no circumstances can it be changed into the moon itself." (An Introduction to Zen Buddhism, 1991) This book popularized Zen Buddhism in the West, but what does Suzuki actually mean by this? There are many interpretations (all valid) of what he means, to start with, he means that the finger can perceive the moon, even if the finger is not the moon itself (or the owner of the finger can), this is a statement of our divided nature in our Samsara, we can perceive, in this life, that we are part of the whole, but we cannot fully identify with the while itself, this is just part of our nature, its limitation if you wish.

It is impossible to simplify Zen teachings, however, there are two concepts that need to be clear:

The belief that our mind is fully enlightened from the beginning and that at some point in our lives we can all reach the realization that we have this fully enlightened mind within ourselves (this is basically the core principle of awakening).

When we awaken and become enlightened, this enlightenment is in itself eternal, but the realization of it only happens within time.

This is why Rinzai Zen, a Japanese school of Zen, places a lot of emphasis on kensho, which we can describe as "insight into our true infinite nature", as we are living within this physical world, we can only have an insight into it, a perception of it, but we cannot fully become one with it, a bit like the finger can never become the moon.

CHAPTER 6

Western Buddhism

If you think that the love affair with Buddhism in the West is a modern phenomenon, you are mistaken, in fact, although Buddhism has only in recent years be-come a very popular spiritual practice in western countries, its origin can be traced back to Alexander the Great, who, whilst conquering Asia Minor, also imported spiritual beliefs from the Orient, the oldest statue of the Buddha known in the west dates back to the first or even second century BCE. Buddhism was known throughout antiquity in the West, not only by the Greeks, but also by the Romans, in fact, Emperor Augustus even witnessed the burning of an Indian religious man in 13 AD (or CE) who wished to demonstrate the strength of his faith, this became a famous incident in the history of the Roman Empire.

There is also strong evidence that Jesus Christ spent years in a Buddhist monastery during the missing years, and it is sure that his teachings had received some influence from Buddhist and Eastern beliefs, for example, in Matthew 6.22, Jesus talk about the Third Eye.

However, when the Roman Empire fell and the Middle Ages began, Buddhism became almost unknown, at least to the common people, and it was only in the nineteenth century that its influence on western philosophy resurfaced, with philosophers like Schopenhauer and Nietzsche. In the late nineteenth century, Helena Blavatsky became an influential figure on popular culture, regarded as the founder of Theosophy, a syncretic spiritual and esoteric study of how all religions and spiritual beliefs seem to have lots of points in common, she is by many regarded as the forerunner of the New Age movement, demonized by the media ever since, her influence on spiritualists all around the world cannot however be denied. This is why the history of Buddhism in the West has been closely connected to the New Age movement, which is arguably the fastest growing (though loosely described) spiritual belief in the West.

However, Buddhism also received a boost in the West through immigration from the East during the twentieth century, in the United Kingdom, for example, there was a massive wave of immigration from India and neighboring countries, with people filling in jobs (especially in the health service and caring industry) that the massive extermination of Britons during the Second World War had left vacant. Buddhism also gained reputation thanks to G.C. Jung, arguably the biggest influence on psychology and psychiatry after S. Freud, who translated The Tibetan Book of the Dead into English in 1927, and who took on many of the teachings of Buddhism in his version of psychology, which has deeply influenced great writers like Virginia Woolf.

It was only in the late 1950s, however, that Buddhism finally took roots with the common people, in particular with texts written by Beat Generation writers such as Kerouac and Alan Watts. With the advent of the hippy phenomenon, Buddhism received yet another boost, the hippies were a revolutionary movement in Europe and in the United States who, disillusioned with the materialistic ways of the West, sought for a deeper truth to the meaning of life by embracing eastern philosophies, including Buddhism. Although the hippy movement has been pronounced dead (this is not true, as many people have been influenced by it and many people still live in hippy communes, and there is even a free town in Europe, Christiania, which is clearly the next stage in the development of the hippy movement, a free anarchist state at the very heart of Copenhagen), its influence has lived on stronger than ever.

The spreading of yoga and meditation in the West is symptomatic of how Buddhism has influenced western societies. There is now virtually no major western city without a Buddhist temple, from California all the way to Australia and New Zealand.

The main forms of Buddhism practiced in the West are Mahayana, Zen and Tibetan Buddhism. However, if one can find a common denominator in Buddhism in the West is its syncretic nature (which goes to the heart of the New Age movement), as we said, syncretism abandons any acceptance of a given dog-ma to find the shared truths of all religions and spiritual beliefs, a word which has become very popular in the West is "awakening", which is of course, a Buddhist concept, it is hard to define what awakening actually means, if not the beginning of the path towards enlightenment. In the West, this awakening is of immense proportions according to statistics (currently about 250 million people are believed to be going through awakening in the West), and it can be triggered by many factors, from spir-itual experiences, to the conscious pursuit of spiritual practices, to a disaffection with the materialist system that governs the West.

Words like Karma and Dharma have now become part of everyday speech in the West, and the future of Buddhism and its influence on western societies is only set to increase in the years to come.

CHAPTER 7

The Noble Truths and How We Interpret Them

We have now seen how Buddhism is practiced around the world, how it has spread and how it has originated, and we have seen the major schools of Buddhism all over the globe. It is now time to look at core concepts of Buddhism in detail and talk about how we can interpret them and live our lives accordingly. It is only fair to start with the four noble truths.

The four noble truths were discovered by the arhat, the followers of the Buddha whom we have seen are regarded as having reached Nirvana. The four noble truths are based on the concept of dukkha, which is actually the first of the noble truths and how to resolve its presence, so, without further ado, here are the four noble truths:

Dukkha, which means "pain", "suffering" and "unsatisfactoriness", dukkha is a natural part of Samsara, as we have seen, but more than being this, it comes from our reaction to the continuous change and impermanent nature of our lives, we want to hold on to things and people, we want to achieve some sort of everlasting happiness in this life, but this is impossible, therefore, if we try to achieve satisfaction and happiness through worldly goods, we are doomed to be dissatisfied by the very nature of this world and our will to resist it.

Samudaya, which is the source of suffering, this is our own de-sire, to hold on to things, be they our wealth, people or our health, it can be seen as our drive to resist the natural state of things, it is closely connected to the principle of tanha, or desire, not only do we desire new things in the hope that they will make us happy, but we also desire what we already have, and when we have to part from them, this is where suffering originates from

Nirodha, which can be translated as "cessation", "annihilation" or "suppression" is the concept that the only way out of suffering is not by rejecting the impermanent nature of things, but by stop-ping our attachment to what we crave for or what we are attached to.

Magga, which is the last of the noble truth, is the eightfold path to enlightenment, the middle way. We have already touched on magga when talking about how the Buddha rejected both indulgence and asceticism in his life on this planet, avoiding the reality of suffering by renouncing everything (or almost everything) that we need to exist in this world is as much an illusion as holding on to it, according to the Buddha, therefore, the middle way, or mag-ga, which accepts that in this Samsara we have to rely on impermanent, mutable phenomena, while also stating that we can de-tach ourselves from them, is the only way. Thus, the middle way opens the door of the eightfold path to enlightenment which we will see more in detail in future chapter.

The Four Noble Truths in Everyday Life

It is important to understand the Buddhism implies a change in the way we perceive life and in the way we conduct ourselves in it, it is not a matter of performing a ritual once a week, as we have already suggested, but a real personal transformation. Realizing how the four noble truths are all pervasive in our lives is therefore very important. As it is hard to come to terms with important events in our lives, maybe it is better to start practicing Buddhism with small things, to "rewire our mind" to this new way of thinking and living.

So, think about something that pleases you a lot, something that triggers your tanha, for example, an ice cream. When you think about an ice cream, you immediately feel an attraction to it if you have a sweet tooth, your connection with the ice cream reaches an apex, a high point, when you are eating it, however, you know quite well that your desire will not be fully satisfied, but only temporarily. Sooner or later, you will be wanting another ice cream, and the cycle of desire and dissatisfaction will start again.

In the modern world, the ice cream we have used as an example can be symbolic of basically everything that we crave, we live in a world where advertisements and the media makes us very, very aware of our cravings; this is how the consumerist system works, by praying on and triggering our desires. Yet we know quite well that we can never satisfy such desires.

So, what is the solution? The solution may be refraining from material things only if our attachment has become pathological (like in serious addictions, which we have already mentioned in this book), but this is not the case for most of us.

This desire comes from a "greedy nature" that we all have, just think about yourself when you go shopping: don't you sometimes want to buy the whole market? Yet we do need to go shopping, because otherwise we would die. So, what is the middle way? The middle way is to change the phrase "I want" with "I need". You need to be fully aware that there are many things you need in your life, and you even have an option, one day, you may decide be-tween apple and pears, we all need fruit to have the vitamins we need to live well, but there are many types of fruit from which we can get them. If you look at the world and what you take from this world in terms of what you need, suddenly, you will discover an abundance that you had never noticed, as your tanha keeps you in an illusion of scarcity. Do you really need the latest phone model, or do you want it, well knowing that a new one will come about soon? But wasn't the old phone more than enough for your needs? By wanting, you feed a sense of scarcity, that nothing is ever enough.

Start doing this with the small things in life, start by never watching advertisements on television, start by shopping according to what you need, and not what you want. Start by eating according to how much you need, and not how much your eyes tell you that you want...

Slowly move to more and more areas of your life. Do you really need that fizzy drink that looks so appetizing? If so, go ahead, but make sure that you actually need it and that it is not just your desire having the best of you. Do you really need that pair of shoes that stare at you saying, "Buy me, buy me!" every time you walk past? If you need a new pair of shoes, by all means buy it, but, again, don't buy it just because it looks good or even worse be-cause it will make you more popular with your friends, even this newly found popularity will only last a few minutes or a few days maximum, then, it will vanish as it has come and you will find yourself craving more popularity, therefore more shoes or whatever gives you this popularity.

The best way to rewire your mind is by making conscious choices based on need and not desire in the little daily actions of our life. It will take time, few people manage to change their whole world view in a matter of weeks or even months, but once this be-comes your new mindset, it will be the way you think even when traumatic losses (like the loss of a loved one) happen in your life.

CHAPTER 8

The Five Precepts and How to Apply Them

At this stage, before we move on to the eightfold way to enlightenment, we should look at the five key ethical rules of Buddhism, these are known in Sanskrit as devangari, or in English as the five precepts of Buddhism. If you come from a western background, you will notice that these five precepts are not that dissimilar from the Ten Commandments, for example (though they are phrased differently and they do not include the worship of a deity).

Remember that you may fail to adhere to the devangari as you start, do not feel upset and angry with yourself about it, we all make mistake, look at whether that was your intention (this is very important) and try to learn from your mistakes.

Do Not Harm Living Things

This is the first of the five precepts, unlike in western religions, where humans are the only beings we should not harm, in Bud-dhism we should not harm any living thing. This is why vegetarian-ism is part and parcel of being a Buddhist, animals, no matter how small, should not be harmed. You may now wonder if killing plants to eat them goes against this rule, as plants too are living things, and Buddhism believes that they too have a soul. Well, the difference between an animal and a plant is that animals are sentient beings, meaning that they can feel pain, emotions and feelings (and we all know that), you can only cause pain to beings that are sentient, beings that are nit sentient will not feel harm, there-fore, you will not hurt them.

This does not mean that you should ill-treat plants, you need to look at them as sharing our world with us, they too deserve respect and care, but they cannot feel pain.

Now, becoming a vegetarian is not easy in many societies, be assured that there is no nutrient that you cannot get from plants, actually, the nutrients in plants are better for us than those in animals (we are by nature herbivores, as we said at the beginning of the book). As with all things, it is better to start step by step, maybe you wish to have a day when you do not eat meat and fish during the week, and keep doing it until you are ready to add another day to your vegetarian diet. Other people have found it helpful to start by only eating meat that is being thrown away by shops, and then have moved on to full vegetarianism. Similarly, keeping in touch with other vegetarians helps too. Feeling good about vegetarian food is also important. People like to take pictures of their vegetarian meals and put them on social media, for example. For most people who have become vegetarians, after a few months, they do not miss meat anymore.

Do Not Take What You Are Not Given

This, of course, includes that you should not steal, that goes without saying. But if you wish, this goes further than that. Ask yourself what exactly we mean by being given… This can lead to deep questions… For example, if you were born in a privileged situation, in a rich country, for example, you were born with privileges that very often were "taken" by one nation from another.

Thus, this precept goes much further than a simple "do not steal", it asks you whether it is fair to buy products that were made in sweatshops, in the end, these are products made with the labor of people who were forced to work to work to give you the Nike shoes, for example. Is this not a way of taking what you are not given?

It also applies to taking credit for someone else's work, the his-tory of the world is full of examples of people who have made a career by taking credit for others, and this culture is very often encouraged on the workplace, surely you know examples of yours of colleagues who took the credit for the work of others. This is something a Buddhist should not do. It may have an impact on your career, especially if you work in a very competitive company, but in the end, you will live better with yourself and, in the end, if your working environment is so designed that it promotes appropriation of ideas, and you are embracing Buddhism, maybe that is not the best place for you to work.

Do Not Engage in Sexual Misconduct

While in some religions sexual misconduct is prescriptive, meaning that there is a rule about what is regarded acceptable and what is not, in Buddhism sexual misconduct is simply based on a simple principle: consent. As long as the people involved in the act are consensual, there is no one else who can tell them that they are doing something wrong.

This, of course, means that gay, lesbian, bisexual and transgender people are never judged by Buddhism, what they do is not sexual misconduct according to Buddhism, because it is con-sensual, while it is for some religions. However, even a small act of imposition of your sexuality on someone else (even a wolf whistle) is regarded as sexual misconduct, if the other person has not consented to it, no matter how small the sexual act is, it is regarded as misconduct.

Do Not Lie and Do Not Gossip

You will notice that this precept adds a layer to what is regarded as unacceptable in some religions and cultures, we all agree that we should not be lying, this seems to be a tenet of all religions, spiritual beliefs and even of atheists, of course, however, Buddhism adds gossip to it. This is very important, because gossip means talking about someone behind this person's back, very often with the intent of hurting her or him, even if not physically (hurting one's reputation, social standing etc. is still hurting).

Should Buddhist read gossip tabloids and the gossip column in magazines? The answer is simply a resounding NO. By doing so, you feed the gossip culture, in the end, no one could gossip if no one would listen to them, gossip needs three agents: the person gossiped about, the person gossiping and the one listening (or reading) the gossip. The first is the victim of gossip, the other two are the perpetrators, with equal responsibility. So, if you are used to reading gossip tabloids and magazines, you will have to change your habits, in the end, there are publications that are so, so much better that there is really no reason to read what is known as "the gutter press".

Are white lies acceptable in Buddhism? That will put you in a very difficult moral position, a white lie is a lie told in order not to hurt someone, therefore, if you want to follow the first precept, sometimes you may have to tell a white lie. Don't make it a habit, though, every time you find yourself in the situation where you think a white lie may be in order, always consider whether it would really hurt the person you are lying to, if it is just to get you off the hook, then it is not a white lie, if it is really to avoid pain to some-one else, then it is a white lie. Do not tell your friends they "look good in that dress" if you know that this lie will have negative re-percussions on them (maybe because he or she will go out in that dress and then suffer from the comments of others), on the other hand, if you know that by not telling the truth, the story will end with you, and the other person will not suffer, then you are entitled to tell a white lie.

Refrain from Taking Intoxicating Substances

This includes not drinking alcohol and not taking intoxicating drugs; anything that may affect our consciousness negatively should be avoided. We live in a world where consciousness is permanently altered, how many coffees do we drink during the day just to keep our mind hyperactive? How many people are taking psychotropic prescription drugs that affect the way their consciousness works?

Now, while monks and nuns will totally refrain from any intoxicating substance, it is clear that for many people it may be difficult to abstain from intoxicating substances, however, if this is your case, maybe because you like the odd glass of wine at the weekend, or because you do know that you drink far too many coffees, you should never be feeling guilty about it. This does not mean that you should not refrain from drinking the odd glass of wine or even smoking the odd spiff, they do affect our mindful-ness therefore our ability to heighten our consciousness. Nevertheless, guilt is a bit like desire, it only leads to dissatisfaction and more craving. Do try to cut down on intoxicating substances, how-ever, which include coffee and, let us not forget, sugar (it too is addictive and causes an altered state of consciousness, and it is actually toxic, thus intoxicating) but remember that no one is judg-ing you if you slip every now and then.

CHAPTER 9

Following the Eightfold Path

We have already talked about the eightfold path at the beginning of this book because it is so fundamental to Buddhism that it is part of its core concepts and practice, in this chapter, we will look at how we can follow it in our lives. Yet, before we do this, let us remind ourselves of what it is, the eightfold path is the way to spiritual enlightenment and it is divided into eight steps in three groups:

- Prajna (wisdom), which includes right view and right re-solve.
- Sila (moral virtue), which includes right speech, right action and right livelihood.
- Samadhi (meditation), which includes right effort, right mindfulness and right concentration.

Achieving right view must be done by understanding Karma, we have seen how this concept has been often confused, sometimes seen as a "cosmic cash machine", it isn't. Understanding that everything we do has a consequence, and that it is in our thoughts and actions that we can influence karmic consequences is a matter of taking responsibility for our thoughts and actions. We are presented with innumerable choices throughout our lives, in fact, at every moment of our life we have a choice. Right view means becoming aware of these choices. The modern world puts such pressure on us that it is sometimes difficult to become aware of these choices, because the next choice is imminent, we lose sight of the one we are asked to make and "skip forward" metaphorically speaking. In order to rewire our mind so that choices become apparent, we need to slow down, we can do this through meditation, or simply by taking things slowly at some times during the day. This can be done with the smallest choices in our lives: which book to read, which television program to watch, whether or not we buy some-thing. If you do this on a regular basis, you will soon notice that even the bigger choices in life become clearer to you. A good way of practicing this is simply by walking: take a walk, but do not decide where you are going (modern life has out destinations to everything we do, even walking), at every single step, look around you and examine the many different options that are given to you. Do this regularly, without having a destination in mind to start with, and you will notice that you have a lot of freedom in life, and it is by using this freedom correctly that you will rewire your mind to achieve right view.

Right resolve can be seen as having the right intentions, we have already talked about how intentions are what matters in Buddhism and for karmic consequences. Modern life has wired our mind so that most of our day is spent in auto-drive, we never pause to think about whether our intentions are noble or not. Yet, as everything that happens in our lives gives us a choice, we are, in fact, asked to use our intentions all the time. Understanding our intentions has become more difficult than what it used to be. You have three options when you are faced with any event in your life: you can do nothing about it, or you can take control and act either way (for or against what has happened). Modern life does not en-courage passivity, in fact, it denigrates it. Yet, it is sometimes our best option, when things are going smoothly, when the universe is not affecting us, what is the point in using our power to intervene? Similarly, if we decide to make a karmic decision, we need to look at what we wish to have as the end result. If the end result is personal benefit, then Karma will be working in the opposite direction. We should always consider the effects of our actions on the whole (as far as we can see) and make a choice that benefits the whole, only this way can we work with Karma and not against it. This too should be practiced with the small things in life: when you buy a pair of shoes, who else is being affected by your decision? Are some children being exploited in a sweat shop somewhere remote from your choice? When you eat a banana, will you be benefiting the farmer (maybe because you have chosen a fair trade banana) or will you be sending money to a big corporation that is exploiting farmers? Ask yourself how far your intentions can affect others (not just people, remember) with the small things in life and you will be rewiring your mind to consider your intentions even with big choices.

Right speech is important, as speech transports emotions, whenever you say something, consider the impact on those who receive your words. We often speak out of frustration or even anger, yet this anger gets transmitted to others, who, in turn may pass it on to other people. You know about this cycle of stress that is repeated over and over again, it often starts at work and penetrates our private lives. Yet, we know that anger calms itself down after a while, so, if you know that your words will carry the vibration of anger, wait a while before you speak.

Right actions goes without saying, whenever we act, we need to consider first the intention of what we do and then the consequences. Sometimes, good intentions have immediate consequences that are negative, this is because people react in a way that we had not envisaged. Well, that is not your problem. If for example you do something which is misinterpreted, or you just make a mistake, and people pick on it, move away from it, do not allow yourself to be drawn into this cycle.

Right livelihood is a big choice in life, many of us want to get more and more in life, but by doing so, we end up taking away from others. Visit a Buddhist temple where monks simply live on alms given by visitors, this is not just a very peaceful experience, but it will help you understand in a practical way how everything we receive is something someone else has either given us, or some-thing we have taken away from them. This needs to be the dividing line: think about where your livelihood comes from someone who is not giving it willingly. This may involve big decisions in life, in these decisions, you need to consider how far you are free, of course, people with a family and who are no longer in their prime will find that making such momentous decisions is not easy for them, however, if you are lucky enough to have all the options open to you, always consider where your livelihood will come from before you accept a job. People who do not advance in their careers are often looked down on by the current system, yet, if this is your best option to live with dignity and not make a karmic decision that will affect others, be strong in your moral choice.

Right effort means that you direct your energy in the correct, moral direction. Monks will usually meditate at the beginning of the day in order to focus their energy on the right direction. If you have no time to focus your energy through meditation in the morning, you can still take a moment, even if it is when you brush your teeth, to pray that the right way is shown to you during the day. An alternative is to pass your hands on your head three times, maybe looking out of the window, and ask for the insight to direct your efforts and energy in a direction that will not harm others.

Right mindfulness is very important, so important, in fact, that we will be dedicating a whole chapter of this book to it. However, at this stage it is important that you understand what mindfulness means, it does not mean "thinking fast" or "thinking sharply", on the contrary, mindfulness means perceiving every sensation to its full, without resisting it. When we think rationally, we isolate our-selves from the universe; we impose our will on all the perceptions we receive, mindfulness means letting go of our ego and allowing the universe to speak to us in its own voice.

Right concentration can be misunderstood, this is because we are brought up to believe that concentration is a somewhat artificial effort to focus on a particular phenomenon, just think about your school days and this will be clear. Yet, by being forced to concentrate on a particular idea, thought, and feeling or in general phenomenon, we do not allow the universe to speak to us. Right concentration, yet again, is achieve by letting go of our desires (including the desire to achieve) and by allowing the universe to direct our concentration where it wishes it to go. For an in-depth discussion on right mindfulness and right concentration, read Chapter 13: 'Bringing Buddhist Mindfulness into Your Life".

CHAPTER 10

The Three Jewels – Wholesome Roots

T he three jewels of Buddhism are the key ideals of Buddhism, they are quite simple, and they are regarded as jewels metaphorically be-cause they shine bright as beacons in our lives, when things be-come difficult, Buddhists are encouraged to take refuge in the three jewels, which are always clear : the Buddha, Dharma and Sangha (which can be translated into "community").

The Buddha

We can always refer to the life of the Buddha for guidance in our lives, but in this context, Buddha also means Buddha nature, you should always believe that you are capable of reaching enlightenment (or that your Buddha nature is inborn within you, de-pending on which school of Buddhism you follow), even in the darkest moments of your life. Be sure of this, and keep following the path that the Buddha has shown us.

Dharma

We have already talked about Dharma, or the teachings of Buddhism, they are here to help us every time we find ourselves in difficulties, this book has explained the teachings of Buddhism in some detail, of course, you can read the original texts (maybe in translation if you can it read Sanskrit), stick to the eightfold path, stick to the four noble truths and to the five precepts of Buddhism. When things become complex, it is sometimes difficult to see the light, it is as if a veil of darkness falls onto our life, however, if you have made the teachings of Buddhism a treasure, they will always shine bright in your life, and they will always show you the right way, even when everything else seems to be covered by clouds.

Sangha

Sangha, as we said, means "community", in the general sense, it means your community (your family, your neighbors and those who share the path with you), however, in this context it means "the community of the enlightened". You will never be turned down by a Buddhist monk or nun (even if you are not a Buddhist), you can always go to them for guidance and to be shown the right path. Sangha is a key jewel, as we are all here to help each other, sometimes, when things become dark in your life, all you need is for someone else to lift the veil of darkness that has fallen in front of your eyes for you. Monks and nuns do this every single days of their lives, in fact, it is one of their main roles in this world. They will not do it out of personal interest, but out of love and compassion and because by lifting this veil, they will do what is tight for you.

Chanting

There are three specific chants that you can use when you need to seek refuge in the three jewels, you can use these if, for example, you cannot seek help from a monk or a nun, you can do this when you have difficulty understanding the Dharma. Chanting works by repeating a sentence over and over again, you need to do it till it the phrase or sentence reaches semantic satiation (which means when it does not seem to make sense anymore, when it becomes devoid of meaning, only then will you have sent the full meaning of the chant into the cosmos), it also needs to be done following your breathing, and with a calm and soothing voice. Here are the chants you can use:

- Buddham saranam gacchami (I seek refuge in the Bud-dha).
- Dhammam sranam gachhami (I seek refuge in the Dharma).
- Sanghan saranam gacchami (I seek refuge in the Sang-ha).

The three jewels are also known as the three wholesome roots, as you can rely on them for your spiritual growth, a bit like a tree relies in its strong and healthy roots to grow, even in winter.

CHAPTER 11

The Three Poisons – Unwholesome Roots

Known in Sanskrit as kleshas, or "afflictions", translated literally into English, the three poisons are part of Samsara, of our physical life, therefore, they are also known as the three unwholesome roots, these start influencing is as soon as we are born, but instead of bringing life, growth and enlightenment to our lives, they bring poi-sons into our lives. These are:

•   Moha (confusion or delusion), it is part of the limited perception of the cosmos that we have whenever we incarnate, in fact, when we incarnate, we lose sight of the deeper spiritual truths of reality and we start being confused by the necessity to lead a physical life. A child, even if he or she has a "sensation" that there is more to his or her life than the material world, will have to focus fully on feeding, then learning the rudiments of this physical reality etc. This divides us from our higher spiritual self. Very often, things happen in our life that push us back into this state of confusion, these may be traumatic events (for example losing your job) or the continuous focus on material wealth of the modern world.

•   Raga (greed or attachment), moha creates an artificial link or attachment to material wealth and possessions, this is so self-evident in the modern world that it needs no explanation. But material wealth, and the greed for it, we know, is only an illusion, it does not give us satisfaction (in fact it creates addiction and even more greed) and it is a substitute for what we all really look for, which is peace. How many wars have been caused by greed, when people only seek peace in their lives?

• Dvdsha (ill intention, ill will, aversion), this comes from our life experiences and perpetuates itself, when we find that we do not like something, instead of letting go of it, we develop a feeling of aversion towards it, next time this happens in our lives, we are already preconditioned to rejecting it, this is at sensory level, yet it transcends into the level of the mind when we start forming negative opinions and we start putting them into action, we start judging people, we start arguing against them without trying to understand them and, in some cases, people start positively acting with the intent to hurt people.

However, these poisons also have metaphorical antidotes, which are respectively prajna (wisdom) or amoha (non delusion), dana (generosity) or alobha (non attachment), metta (love and kindness) and advesa (non hatred). As you can see, there are two antidotes for each poison; one is neutral, and it simply means re-fraining from using the poison, the other is positive, and it means using the opposite quality to neutralize the poison itself. The karmic power of these antidotes cannot be stressed enough. Think about a little incident in your life, maybe just a small argument with a friend which you did not understand (moha) and, first of all, distance yourself from it (amoha), then try to look at the argument from your friend's perspective and with the intention not to find what is wrong with it, but the points that your friend was right about. Finally, ask yourself what a wise person would do (not an intelligent one, but a wise one): wouldn't the wise person tell your friend that he or she was right on those points?

CHAPTER 12

The Modern Buddhist

Being a Buddhist in the modern world, especially in the West, has challenges, but ironically, the very challenges that modern life presents us in leading a life as a Buddhist are also the very reasons and motivations that people have to be Buddhists. This may sound contradictory, but if we look at some of the main challenges you will see how, within each of them, there is the very reason to follow Buddhism.

As we have seen, Buddhism has been around for more than two millennia so far, so, being a Buddhist now in a way means following an oath that was set a very, very long time ago (which-ever school or practice you decide to embrace), on the other hand, the world has changed so much since the times of the Buddha, that there are, of course, specific challenges that are brought about by living in a modern society.

Contact with Nature

By nature, we do not just mean flowers, plants animals, rivers and mountains, but the very transcendental essence of nature. Nowadays, however, many people are so detached from the natural world that they are seldom in touch with its physical dimension, let alone its spiritual one. We are not just talking about the fact that many of us lived "boxed up" in flats surrounded by other flats and then miles of grey concrete, we are also referring to the fact that we now are subjected to what humankind has produced much more often and consistently than what nature offers us, we could call this the "virtual reality" of the television, the internet, the social media etc. These are all human constructs, and they keep us separate from nature and its spirit.

Even the food we eat is no longer, in many cases, natural at all, this is more true in the USA than in other countries, but it is true to a certain degree at least in the vast majority of western countries (and now some eastern ones too).

Yet, people have an innate need to be in touch with nature, this is why, when we have a few hours to spare, many of us feel the need to go to a park, to go away from the artificial environment that we have created for ourselves and rediscover our own "umbilical cord" with mother nature. Translated into spiritual practice, Buddhism offers a contact with the transcendental essence of nature that is daily, direct and very strong. In fact, if you ask any-body to close their eyes and think about Buddhism, the chances are that words like "trees" and "flowers" will soon come to mind.

As a little tip, though not strictly Buddhist, have you ever heard of the barefoot revolution? If you haven't think about how we modern people spend virtually all our lives with our feet divided from the soul by plastic, rubber or sometimes leather, this creates an artificial barrier between our being and the very energy of nature. Try to take a barefoot walk in a park or on a beach as often as you can, this has been demonstrated to have very positive effects on your energy (we become like lightning rods and ions from the ground travel up and out into the air, man effect similar to when we meditate near a waterfall).

Tolerance

Do we live in a tolerant society? Well, this may depend a bit on the country you live in, your community and what we mean by "tolerant". While on the one hand there is a push towards a more tolerant society in many countries around the world, on the other there is the exact opposite reaction, let us look at the recent discussion on LGBT rights in the USA, it all happened with a bit of a fight, on the one hand, there were those who just could not see why LGBT people should not get married, on the other hand, there were those who felt threatened by it. Of course, tolerance is a key value of Buddhism, this may have implications in the positions you take on social matters. Is this world looking after its most vulnerable individuals? Hardly so. In fact, while being LGBT in a rich country may now give you the same rights as being straight, there are still many people who are starving and have no access to even water in the world. Being able to see the whole world (and the universe, but at this stage let us focus on this world, there is plenty to do!) as a whole is the very key to tolerance. This, however, is not how social change tends to work, it tends to work through "neighbors", meaning that we tend to spread love to those nearer to us and forget those who are further away (from where we live or from our view). Being a Buddhist also means looking out for the very people that society has forgotten, the very poor, the downtrodden, and the pariahs of the world. Everybody deserves peace, love, dignity and our respect, even those we do not know and do not under-stand.

Religious Diversity

In many countries, religious diversity is accepted, but it does not mean that there is no tension, it is easy to see this when we think about how many Muslims are demonized in western societies, while they have a right to practice, they are often treated as "aliens" nevertheless. Buddhists do not receive this treatment in such societies, maybe because of geopolitical reasons, or because, as we said, Buddhism is not actually a religion. However, a Buddhist should promote religious tolerance even towards other spiritual beliefs. Buddhists are non-proselytizers, meaning that we do not go round trying to find new "believers" (unlike some religions), nevertheless, we should encourage tolerance and understanding of other spiritual faiths, even if that seems, on the surface, to go against "our interests", in fact our interest is the wellbeing and enlightenment of everybody, whichever path they choose.

Nonviolence

Nonviolence is at the very core of Buddhism, it is difficult, nowadays, not to be tempted into violent behavior, this does not just mean directly, but also indirectly, meaning by promoting violence by proxy (supporting wars, for example). While it is unthinkable that anyone reading this book will ever commit direct violence on a fellow human being (and hopefully not on animals too), he modern world is so radicalized (meaning that positions have become entrenched) that many of us may live in country currently or recently at war with another country. Although it is understand-able that if you are not a leader of your country your say in this will be limited, you still have a duty, as a Buddhist, to do every-thing you can to prevent violence, even violence committed by your country against another country in your name.

Materialism

This is a big, big point. "We live in a material world" ironically sang a hit in the 80s, when the materialist world view became all powerful, we are invited (one would say coerced) to chase material wealth throughout our lives, as we have seen, this only leads to more craving and more dissatisfaction, not only, but this system is keeping other people in a state of abject poverty, this clearly goes against the precepts of Buddhism. Stepping outside the materialist world view is the very first thing a Buddhist should do in the mod-ern world to start the journey towards enlightenment. It is a very important step, sometimes even a difficult one. It may involve changing your daily actions, even changing your job if you can (note: if you can, we are not suggesting that you do if it is impossible). Living in balance with the universe also means living in balance with society. So many of us are in parasitic jobs (maybe being a banker is not the ideal career for a Buddhist), in parasitic lives that depend on taking rom others. As a Buddhist, you should be seeking a way out of this, even if it starts with a compromise (which may just mean that you will not go for a promotion that will lead to more money, more material wealth and more dissatisfaction as a consequence of being further into this cycle).

Generosity

It is important that you are generous in the modern world, just giving to the odd charity, hoping that they will take a moral weight off your shoulders then walking past the homeless person on the street in need of food is not enough. If your pockets are empty, exchange a word, a smile, a sign of recognition (a blessing in particular), if you have something to spare, give for the joy and beau-ty of giving, never expecting anything back in return, not even a thank you. If you have some spare time (something which is be-coming a rarity in the modern world), why don't you consider doing some charitable work? Why don't you spend some time giving your energy, if you do not have material resources, to others? Giving is at the heart of Buddhism and modern society, built on greed and selfishness, is really full of opportunities to give at every corner.

CHAPTER 13

Bringing Buddhist Mindfulness into Your Life

Mindfulness is a state of mind, this seems simple, but it actually is not as easy as it seems, in many cultures, the mind is seen mainly as a process, and it is often identified with rationality. Although reason is part of our mind, more one of its processes, it is not the mind itself. Mindfulness is maybe better understood as a state where your mind is at one with the objects of your senses, we eat fast, we drink fast, we do everything without giving our mind to the very actions and phenomena we encounter in our lives, this is not being mindful.

In order to be mindful, you need to allow the very senses to speak to you freely, without imposing your preconceived ideas on it, think about it with a simple example: even before you eat a fruit, you already have an idea about how the fruit should taste, smell and feel. How can the fruit speak to your senses if you already activate your senses even before you eat it? In order to be mindful, therefore, you need to let go of your ego and feel fully. There are many ways with which you can bring Buddhist mindfulness into your life, it is again a matter of rewiring your brain so that it is naturally in a mindful state and two of the main ways are by small daily actions and by meditating.

Daily Actions

We will now look at some simple exercises to bring mindfulness into your life. First, choose a nice sunny day, go to the park or to the beach... Take off your shoes, slowly, and start feeling your feet relax, feel the warmth of your feet mix with the crisp freshness of the air caressing them, do this slowly, do not rush it, allow for the sensation to have told you everything it can possibly tell you before moving in to the next stage. Now put your feet to the ground, feel the contact with the soil, with the blades of grass, with the leaves on the ground, do not hurry this, do not force your weight onto the ground. Just allow the blades of grass, the ground, and the leaves to talk to your feet naturally, at their own pace, and with their own essence. It is not your feet against them, but your feet with them. Next rest your feet on the ground, feel them share temperature, moisture and if you can energy with the ground itself. Again, take it slowly, allow the ground to lead you and do not force yourself onto it.

Next, feel the energy (warmth, texture, moisture) of the ground slowly rise into your legs, feel it become part if you, sharing with you its own very essence, feel this energy climb up your calves, then your thighs and let it move inside your being at ease, do not force it in any direction and do not impose any speed on it, abandon yourself completely to the ground. Feel it rise into your body, again, at its own speed, without forcing it but always welcoming it. If you do this repeatedly and regularly, you will reach a point when you can actually taste and smell the ground. After the exercise, breathe out, feeling the energy of the ground leave you softly and mix with the air.

Now, let us start from the other end, pick a fruit and look at it, nit with greed, not with the desire to "devour it", but simply to get to know it, feel it in your hands, feel its texture, how soft or hard it is, if it is smooth, or rough or velvety. Slowly bring it to your mouth and pause as soon as you can smell it, allow its scent to enter you and travel from your nose down inside your body. Then, touch the fruit with your lips, as if kissing it, just feel its consistency, its texture, its smell with your lips. At this stage, you may even be able to taste it already. Slowly bring it into your mouth and hold it there, do not bite it yet, but allow it to make its presence felt inside of you. After this, bite it slowly and feel its juices on your tongue and on your palate, allow them to become part of your mouth, to tell you whatever they wish to tell you. As you do so, you may start feeling the energy of the fruit becoming part of you, flowing down with all its flavor, with its aroma, its temperature and its texture inside of you. Do not push it, but follow it as deep into your body as you can, even all the way down to your feet. Finally, swallow the fruit slowly, and follow it down inside of you as it becomes part of you. After this, breathe out and feel your being sharing the fruit with the air around you through your breath.

You will need to repeat these simple exercises frequently and regularly, and you will notice that, by following the sensations that the world gives you, your mind will become more still and at the same time more aware. You can, of course, adapt these exercises for everything, from stroking a cat to drinking water or wearing a hat.

Meditation

We have seen how meditation is very important in Buddhism, in fact, Buddhism has developed many different forms of meditation, with different functions and positions. Meditation calms the mind, and it has many positive effects on people's spiritual, mental and even physical health. In this chapter, we will look at how you can use meditation to increase your mindfulness, which is certainly (as you can see from the eightfold path) an important step on your way to spiritual enlightenment. Although when people think about meditation the first thing that often comes to mind is the lotus position, that is a very, very advanced meditation position, in fact, if you are new to it, you should not even try it, as you risk dislocating one of your femurs. Instead, we will look at the key principles of mindful meditation.

The idea of meditation is to silence the ego, which is that voice at the back of your mind, that chatter, that virtually never stops talking, and which can keep people awake at night.

There is no prescribed position to meditate, contrary to popular belief, the important thing is that you feel fully at ease and that your spine is straight. This means that you have to choose a place that is not noisy, not crowded, which gives you "good vibes" (it can be indoors or outdoors), you must wear comfortable clothes, and you should do it at a time when your mind is not distracted by other engagements (some people can, because they are experienced, do it before they go to work, but the average person would be worrying about the day ahead so much that the meditation may not work, therefore, the best times to start meditating are in the evening or at the weekend if you are new to it). You should also do it when you are not hungry, but also when you do not feel "too full", if you have had a heavy meal, the chances are that you will fall asleep. Make sure that no one disturbs you when you are meditating, if you have small children, this may be difficult, maybe ask your partner to look after them for the time you are meditating. You should meditate for at least twenty minutes in each session.

First of all, you need to learn to belly breathe, think about a baby, when a baby breathes, you see her or his belly swelling and then going down, this is because babies, like singers, belly breathe, then at about the age of five, we forget how to belly breathe, and we only do it when we sleep. Belly breathing allows you to breathe in much more air than chest breathing. So, instead of pushing your ribcage out when you breathe, push your diaphragm down and your stomach out, fill the lungs by pushing the air down, as if they were pistons, rather than to the side. Practice this a few time before you meditate, so you know how to do it, it usually does not take long.

Once you know how to belly breathe, you can start meditating. Found a comfortable place and time? Found a comfortable position with your spine straight? Good, now close your eyes (don't force them, just close them softly). With your eyes closed, focus your eyes (still closed) just about three feet in front of you and to the level of your knees (if you are sitting down, this would be on the ground), you will be basically focusing in front of you and down, allow this focus to be loose, do not force it if it wonders a bit, it's perfectly fine.

Now, breathe in, slowly with your nose, hold the air in for a second or two, and breathe out. You will hear your ego talking, it is like a chatter that reminds you of all your engagements, of your ideas, of what you are worried about etc. This is what you will need to silence, stop paying attention to it and focus on your breathing. It may take some time, but if you focus on your breathing, on its sound and on how it feels, this voice from the back of your mind will finally go silent, it will go silent more easily and faster the more you practice meditation. When this voice has silenced, you are practicing meditation.

Instead of focusing on a specific object, feeling or idea(this can be done in meditation too), just allow your senses to guide you, if you feel a little breeze, just allow it to "talk to you" metaphorically speaking, if you feel the warmth of the sun on your skin, allow it to "talk to you" metaphorically speaking, just keep focusing on your breathing and allow your mind to be guided by the "external world" rather than using it to "decipher and analyze" every phenomenon that happens to be in contact with your mind. Just feel, do not think.

You may need to try it a few times before it actually works for you but don't give up. It is a good idea to practice mindful meditation regularly, at least once a week (which given the busy lives some of us lead, it is as far as we can), but ideally every day. You will be rewiring your mind to accept rather than analyze the world, and you will soon start to notice that, apart from being generally more peaceful and calm, you will be more mindful even when you are not meditating.

CHAPTER 14

Buddhist Concepts and Practices

We have come to the end of this long journey, but this is just the beginning. Hopefully, this book will be, for some of you, the very first step to the path to enlightenment, it is a long path, but it gets brighter and brighter as you walk along. In this chapter, we will be making the point on some of the key Buddhist principles and practices, so that you can always refer to them on the way to awakening and spiritual enlightenment.

Key Buddhist Practices

Here are some key Buddhist practices for you:

• Meditation: we have seen how meditation is a core practice of Buddhism, in fact, Buddhism has developed many different ways of meditating and for many different purposes. When people think about meditation, most of them conjure up the image of the lotus position, in fact, that is a very advanced position, and you should not be attempting it if you are new to meditation, or you may risk dislocating a femur. We have, however, seen how you can use meditation to increase your mindfulness. You can also use meditation to focus on an idea, a phenomenon or a feeling: if you decide to do so, do not apply your knowledge, your rational understanding of this idea, feeling or phenomenon to it, instead allow it to metaphorically speak to you freely, follow it wherever it leads you: you have nothing to fear. For example, you may wish to meditate at sunrise, in which case, allow the sun to lead you in the experience, do not start thinking about what will or may happen, and do not apply your knowledge of astronomy to the experience. Similarly, you may want to meditate by the waves of the ocean (which is a beautiful experience), if you do so, do not analyze rationally how the waves are formed and what brings them onto the shore, allow their rhythm, their sound, the smells they bring to you to guide you along the way. Meditating means becoming one with the object of our meditation, and this cannot happen if we impose our preconceived ideas onto it. You should meditate very regularly, at least once a week (which is as far as some people with very busy lives can afford), but ideally, you should meditate daily.

• Prayers: we have seen how prayers are important in Buddhism, but we have also seen that prayers do not need to be directed towards a deity, praying in Buddhism simply means speaking to the universe, you can do this in your own way, with your own words, you do not need any formulas to follow. You should pray regularly, even if for a short time, you should pray daily. You can just direct your feelings and thoughts to the universe, share what you think and feel with the whole, and that is a prayer.

• Chanting mantras: we have seen how chanting is important in Buddhism, chanting works by letting go of the rational meaning attached to the words we chant, this only happens when we r and over again until it is only sound, until it ceases to make sense rationally (and beyond this point), do it in harmony with your breathing, softly and repetitively, this is the only way that chanting works.

• Vegetarianism: if you are not a vegetarian, and you are only now beginning to approach this lifestyle, it may look daunting at the start. However, you should be confident in the fact that every time you go shopping and you choose not to buy meat, you also choose not to hurt a sentient being. In the next chapter, you will find some resources that will help you with your motivation and with becoming a vegetarian. Take this step by step, and you will soon find that meat and fish no longer appeal to you.

• Giving: giving for the sake of giving, without expecting anything in return is a core practice of Buddhism. Giving does not mean just giving money, wealth or material goods, it also means giving your time, your blessings, your human and humane contact: next time you walk past a homeless person on the pavement, even if you do not have any money to spare, stop by and exchange a smile and a few words.

• Nonviolence: nonviolence is a way of living, it involves every decision we make in our lives, surely, if you have read this book so far, you will already have a nonviolent nature, however, remember that nonviolence also means doing everything in your power to stop violence in your name and violence from others. In the next chapter, you will find some in depth resources on what nonviolence actually means in our daily lives.

•   Blessing: blessing is a very powerful act, it means sharing your energy with someone or something else, you can bless anything and anybody, even the universe itself, by doing so, you will be opening up a channel of energy with what or whom you bless, this is a two way system, you will be giving energy and at the same time receiving fresh energy: it is a win-win situation. If energy is enclosed in a system, you will find that it becomes stagnant, the beauty of energy is that the more we share it, the more it rejuvenates. Start by blessing the universe every night before you go to bed, you will wake up happier, stronger and more energetic.

•   Burning candles and incense: we have seen how in some forms of Buddhism, burning candles and incense is regarded as a way of becoming closer to the spiritual world, there are so many aromas available nowadays that the choice is enormous, burning incense and candles will bring peace into your life, but also into the whole universe.

Core Concepts of Buddhism

Here is a list of the core concepts of Buddhism, which you can use as a reference:

•   Arhat: an enlightened being who has achieved a state of Nirvana.
•   Atoms of Existence: these are the true elements of the physical and natural world.

• Bodhisattva: this is an enlightened being, an arhat, who chooses to remain in the cycle in order to teach and guide other beings on their path to Nirvana.

• Cycle of Rebirth (Samsara): the endless cycle of reincarnation of all sentient beings.

• Emptiness: this is the inescapable condition of fleeting impermanence of all composites of atoms, of all phenomena and of all things, the essential quality of our physical existence.

• Enlightenment (bodhi): this is the awakening to the awareness of one's ignorance of the reality of the spiritual realm.

• Ignorance: this is the realization and belief that phenomena and things are actually real and permanent, this is the illusion that anchors sentient beings in the cycle of rebirth and suffering, the desiring and craving to preserve one's self as a physical being and to possess things.

• Karma: this is the cosmic law that regulates how our mental acts (which can then be translated into actions, but do not necessarily have to, this is why intentions are fundamental in Buddhism) have an effect on increasing or decreasing ignorance or enlightenment.

• Mahayana Buddhism: the schools of Buddhism which see the Boddhisattva as the ideal (the major form of Buddhism in China, Korea, and Japan, the most common Buddhist school).

• Mental Concentration: this is the he first step to perceiving clearly.

• Nirvana: the state of annihilation, end and extinction of the illusory self in a clear perception of the illusion and emptiness of existence, it comes with the merging of consciousness with the wholeness and oneness of reality, it is the withdrawal from cycle of rebirth.

• Pure Consciousness, Thoughts and Mind: these are the three levels of mental activity: an existing flow of sentience, atom based thoughts and perceptions, the intellect.

• Selfhood: the belief (mistaken) that we have a permanent identity, often identified with the mind and its mechanisms, like rational thinking.

• Soul (atman): this is the core of the self erroneously identified with mental activity.

• The Eightfold Path: eight steps in three groups: 1)

• The Five Skandhas: these are the five elements which join to form the illusory identity of a human being: 1) material form, 2) feelings, 3) perceptions, 4) impulses, 5) consciousness.

• The Four Noble Truths: 1) life in Samsara is always causing suffering, 2) this has a cause, 3) this can ended, 4) there is a path (eightfold path) shown by the Buddha for ending it.

• Theravada (also known as Hinayana) Buddhism: this is the group of Buddhist schools which take the Arhat as the ideal (currently most popular in Southeast Asia).

• Trance (dhyana, or Zen in Japanese): This is the state of the mind as it truly perceives, not conditioned by the illusion of division.

• Wisdom (prajna): this occurs when we have a clear perception of the world as emptiness and as a sensory illusion.

Further Reading (Reference Links)

As promised, here are some very useful links and books to help you along the path.

A comprehensive guide to Buddhism:

https://thebuddhistcentre.com/buddhism

Classes and courses on Buddhism:

http://www.thebuddhistsociety.org/

A simple guide to Buddhism:

http://www.aboutbuddhism.org/

A short but comprehensive life of the Buddha:

http://www.souledout.org/wesak/storybuddha.html

A documentary on the life of the Buddha:

https://www.youtube.com/watch?v=FT6FcIXxE8E

A cartoon on the life of the Buddha (for children and adults):

https://www.youtube.com/watch?v=Nw5YRPn8KYI

A very long cartoon on the life of the Buddha (again, for children and adults alike):

https://www.youtube.com/watch?v=9oh6BaESLbs

A list of Buddhist mantras and their meanings:

http://www.wildmind.org/mantras/figures

Some videos on how to recite Buddhist mantras:

http://www.freemeditationinfo.com/meditation-instructions/buddhist-mantras.html

Free MP3 downloads of Buddhist mantras:

http://junglevibe2.net/tracks/buddhist_mantra.html

Do you want to find a Buddhist temple near you? Just type in your postcode:

http://buddhism.about.com/od/findingatempleandsangha/

20 practical Zen meditation techniques:

http://zenhabits.net/meditation-guide/

A free guide to meditation:

http://marc.ucla.edu/body.cfm?id=22

Nonviolence explained for you:

http://www.nonviolenceinternational.net/seasia/whatis/book.php

Help on becoming a vegetarian:

https://www.vegsoc.org/definition

If you need some motivation in becoming a vegetarian, watch this speech (warning, it is very strong):

https://www.youtube.com/watch?v=es6U00LMmC4

Made in the USA
San Bernardino, CA
03 July 2017